THE DECLARATION OF INDEPENDENCE

BY MELISSA McDANIEL

CHILDREN'S PRESS®
An Imprint of Scholastic Inc.
New York Toronto London Auckland Sydney
Mexico City New Delhi Hong Kong
Danbury, Connecticut

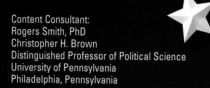

BRINGING HISTORY to LIFE

Content Consultant:
Rogers Smith, PhD
Christopher H. Brown
Distinguished Professor of Political Science
University of Pennsylvania
Philadelphia, Pennsylvania

Library of Congress Cataloging-in-Publication Data
McDaniel, Melissa, 1964–
   The Declaration of Independence/by Melissa McDaniel.
      p. cm.—(Cornerstones of freedom)
   Includes bibliographical references and index.
   ISBN-13: 978-0-531-25030-3 (lib. bdg.)   ISBN-10: 0-531-25030-X (lib. bdg.)
   ISBN-13: 978-0-531-26555-0 (pbk.)   ISBN-10: 0-531-26555-2 (pbk.)
   1. United States. Declaration of Independence–Juvenile literature.
   2. United States—Politics and government—1775–1783—Juvenile
   literature.
   I. Title. II. Series.
   E221.M38 2012
   973.3'13—dc22   2011012329

Photographs © 2012: Alamy Images: 54 (BL Images Ltd), 37 (North
Wind Picture Archives); AP Images: 14, 59 left (Alonzo Chappel/North
Wind Picture Archives), 12 (Darley/North Wind Picture Archives), 11,
16, 23, 30, 32, 34, 38, 42, 44, 59 right (North Wind Picture Archives), 47
(Bela Szandelszky), back cover (Mark Wilson); Bridgeman Art Library
International Ltd., London/New York: 26, 56 top (Sir Godfrey Kneller/Private
Collection/Photo ©Philip Mould Ltd, London), 40 (Private Collection/Peter
Newark American Pictures), 25 (Howard Pyle/Delaware Art Museum,
Wilmington); Getty Images/William Barnes Wollen/Hulton Archive:
19; iStockphoto/John Clines: cover; Library of Congress: 18, 56 bottom
(John Singleton Copley/Museum of Fine Arts, Boston), 35 (Clyde Deland/
Harper's Weekly), 24 (Jean Leon Gerome Ferris/The Foundation Press,
Inc., Cleveland), 13 (William Hoare), 29, 57 (Gilbert Stuart), 27; Melissa
McDaniel: 64; ShutterStock, Inc.: 41, 51 (Susan Law Cain), 55 (gary718);
Superstock, Inc.: 4 bottom, 22 (Alonzo Chappel/Universal Images Group),
36 (Henry Alexander Ogden), 28 (John Trumbull); The Granger Collection,
New York: 2, 3, 46 (Charles Willson Peale), 4 top, 5 left, 5 right, 6, 10, 15, 20,
33, 39, 48, 49, 50, 58; The Image Works/Iberfoto: 8.

Did you know that studying history can be fun?

BRING HISTORY TO LIFE by becoming a history investigator. Examine the evidence (primary and secondary source materials); cross-examine the people and witnesses. Take a look at what was happening at the time—but be careful! What happened years ago might suddenly become incredibly interesting and change the way you think!

Contents

SETTING THE SCENE
"If This Be Treason" 6

CHAPTER 1
Toward a New Nation.....8

CHAPTER 2
"Free and Independent States" 20

CHAPTER 3
Inside the Declaration. 30

CHAPTER 4
Spreading the News 42

MAP OF THE EVENTS
What Happened Where?....................52

THE STORY CONTINUES
A Gift to the Future...... 54

Influential Individuals 56
Timeline 58
Living History 60
Resources 6 1
Glossary 62
Index............................63
About the Author...............64

A MONUMENTAL INSCRIPTION

ON THE

Fifth of March.

Together with a few LINES

On the Enlargement of

EBENEZER RICHARDSON,

Convicted of MURDER.

"If This Be Treason"

Patrick Henry's words inspired the American colonists to begin a revolution against Great Britain.

On May 29, 1765, 29-year-old Patrick Henry rose from his seat in the Virginia **Assembly** to speak. He spoke out sharply against the Stamp Act, a tax the British **Parliament**

IN 1775, PATRICK HENRY SAID,

had recently imposed on the American **colonists**. The colonists did not send representatives to Parliament, he argued, and therefore had no one in England to stand up for their interests.

Henry's harsh words convinced the members of the assembly to pass a **resolution** stating that only colonial assemblies had the right to impose taxes in the colonies. Some members of the assembly thought this idea was outrageous. They thought Henry was attacking the British king, George III. "**Treason**!" they called out. According to some accounts, Henry replied, "If this be treason, make the most of it!"

News of Henry's speech spread like wildfire through the American colonies. Never before had colonists made such an open attack on British rule. Henry's speech and the Virginia resolution were among the earliest rumblings of the coming American Revolutionary War.

The British believed they had the right to govern their American colonies as they wanted. As years passed, Parliament imposed more taxes and passed laws that frustrated the colonists because they had no representation. Tempers on both sides were rising, and violent conflict was on its way.

CHAPTER 1

TOWARD A NEW NATION

By the mid-1700s, the American colonies were filled with thriving cities.

IN THE 1600S, ENGLISH MEN, women, and children began heading west across the Atlantic Ocean to the coast of North America. Some came for the land. Others came seeking religious freedom that they did not have at home. By the middle of the 1700s, a string of 13 English colonies had been established along the Atlantic coast.

Not all of the 2.5 million people who lived in the colonies were English. About half a million people were of African descent and had been brought to North America as slaves. Many others were Dutch and German. But regardless of their background, they were all British subjects. Great Britain's government, as well as most of the colonists themselves, expected the Americans to be loyal to the king.

The king appointed royal governors to oversee each colony. Although each colony had an assembly to make its own laws, the king could **veto** the laws. Most of the time, however, the colonists made laws without British interference.

The French and Indian War gave Great Britain control of the North American continent.

An Expensive War

Britain was not the only European nation that had colonies in North America. The French controlled much of what is now Canada and the central United States. As British colonists pushed westward, they came into conflict with the French. The two powers fought for control of North America. This conflict, known as the French and Indian War, or Seven Years' War, began in 1754. Great Britain finally won the war in 1763, but waging the long conflict was very costly.

Providing the army and forts necessary to protect American colonists and fight the war left Britain deeply in **debt**. To raise money to pay the debt, the British began imposing taxes on the colonists. Americans began to fume.

Taxation without Representation

In 1765, Parliament passed the Stamp Act, which required colonists to buy a stamp to put on every piece of printed material they used. The act taxed newspapers, legal documents, playing cards, calendars, and many other items.

Most colonists opposed the Stamp Act.

THE FOLLY OF ENGLAND AND THE RUIN OF AMERICA

Stamp Act protests sometimes turned violent.

Colonists began to protest and resist British authority. Some merchants refused to buy British goods. Many women stopped buying British cloth. Instead, they made their own. In Boston, Massachusetts, people organized demonstrations against the Stamp Act. One of these demonstrations turned into a riot, with the crowd attacking a stamp distributor's home. A **boycott** of British goods convinced Parliament to **repeal** the Stamp Act in 1766.

But the British still believed they had the right to govern the colonies as they wanted. "This [Great Britain] is the Mother Country," proclaimed William Pitt, an important British politician. "They [the colonists] are the children. They must obey."

More taxes followed. The British taxed paper and glass, paint and tea. Once more, the colonists protested and boycotted. Once more, the British backed down, repealing most of the taxes.

William Pitt and other British politicians believed that the colonists had no right to protest the taxes imposed by Britain.

The First Shots

The British sent troops to the colonies to help keep order in the cities that had seen the most protests. Nowhere was there more fiery resistance than in Boston. On March 5, 1770, a large group of Bostonians began hurling insults at a small group of British soldiers.

The Boston Massacre became a major scandal in the colonies.

The colonists put rocks inside snowballs and lobbed them toward the **Redcoats**, the British soldiers. In the confusion, the frightened soldiers fired into the crowd. They accidentally killed five Bostonians, including a black sailor named Crispus Attucks.

News of the attack raced through the colonies. Many Americans believed that the Bostonians had been murdered. The colonists called it the Boston Massacre.

YESTERDAY'S HEADLINES

In the 1700s, newspapers and **broadsides** were the main way of spreading information. In the aftermath of the Boston Massacre, a broadside was printed about one of the British soldiers, Ebenezer Richardson. It read:

> Awake my drowsy thoughts! Awake my muse!
> Awake O earth, and tremble at the news!
> In grand defiance to the laws of God,
> The guilty, guilty murd'rer walks abroad.
> That city mourns, (the cry comes from the ground,)
> Where law and justice never can be found
> Oh! sword of vengeance, fall thou on the race
> Of those who hinder justice from its place.
> O MURD'RER! Richardson! with their latest breath
> Millions will curse you when you sleep in death!

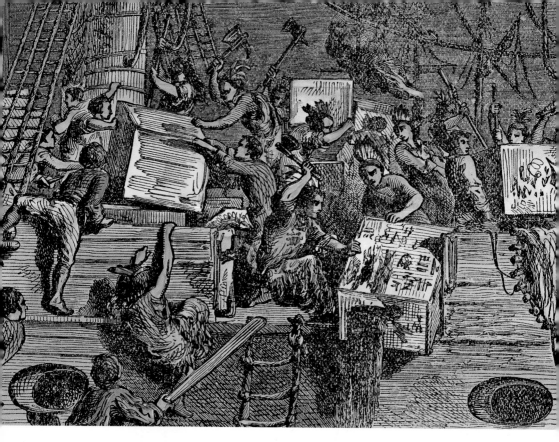

The colonists destroyed thousands of pounds of tea during the Boston Tea Party.

"Boston Harbor a Teapot Tonight!"

The British had repealed the taxes on many goods, such as paper and glass, but they had not repealed the taxes on tea. Tea was a favorite beverage of the colonists, and they strongly opposed the tax. Many refused to buy British tea. When British ships bearing cargoes of tea arrived at American ports, colonists refused to unload them. Some ships turned back and sailed home across the Atlantic. But in 1773, three ships filled with tea sat in Boston Harbor. The royal governor of Massachusetts refused to let them leave until the tea was unloaded.

Samuel Adams, a cousin of future president John Adams, began planning a way to use the ships to demonstrate the colonists' growing frustrations. On the night of December 16, 1773, dozens of men and boys dressed as Native Americans boarded the ships with shouts of "Boston harbor a teapot tonight!" They emptied all 342 chests of tea into the frigid harbor waters. On shore, colonists looked on with mixed feelings at the event that would come to be known as the Boston Tea Party.

The British were outraged by the actions of the colonists. King George wanted to punish the people of Massachusetts, and Parliament passed a series of laws the Americans called the **Intolerable** Acts. The colony was placed under military rule. No longer would the people of Massachusetts be allowed to govern themselves. Soldiers were sent into Boston, and the colonists were required to house them. Boston Harbor was closed until the colony paid for all the tea that had been destroyed.

A FIRSTHAND LOOK AT
THE *BOSTON TEA PARTY*

In 1789, an engraving titled *Boston Tea Party* appeared in *The History of North America*, a book published in London, England, 16 years after the event. The artist, W. D. Cooper, labeled his illustration "Americans throwing the Cargoes of the Tea Ships into the River, at Boston." See page 60 for a link to view the print.

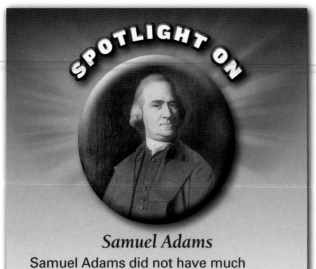
Samuel Adams

Samuel Adams did not have much success early in life. He studied law, but not for long. He worked as a tax collector, but he seldom collected any money. Adams was passionate about politics, however, and he soon learned what his true skills were. He helped plan the Boston Tea Party and organize resistance to the Intolerable Acts. He became a leader of the people opposing the British, and one of the most important voices in the colonies. Some people said he was a troublemaker and a fanatic, but Thomas Jefferson called him "truly the Man of the Revolution."

Into Battle

Leaders from 12 of the 13 colonies met in Philadelphia, Pennsylvania, in September 1774. They called themselves the Continental Congress. Some colonial **delegates** believed that war with Great Britain was soon coming. Others hoped to avoid conflict and work with the king and Parliament to resolve the growing tensions.

The Continental Congress drafted a letter to King George, asking that the colonists be given the same rights as Englishmen. King George ignored the letter, and revolution came a step closer. People in the colonies began preparing for battle. They gathered weapons and made plans to defend themselves.

In April 1775, about 700 British troops marched out of Boston toward the nearby town of Concord. Their goal was to capture weapons that were hidden there.

The colonial fighters stood their ground against the Redcoats at Lexington.

But before the Redcoats got to Concord, they arrived in the town of Lexington. About 70 colonial troops had gathered in the center of town with whatever weapons they could find.

Their leader, Captain John Parker, told them, "Stand your ground. Don't fire unless fired upon. But, if they want to have a war, let it begin here!"

The colonial soldiers stood in the way of the advancing Redcoats. No one knows who fired the first shot, but in less than one minute, eight Americans lay dead. The British were soon marching toward Concord. The American Revolutionary War had begun.

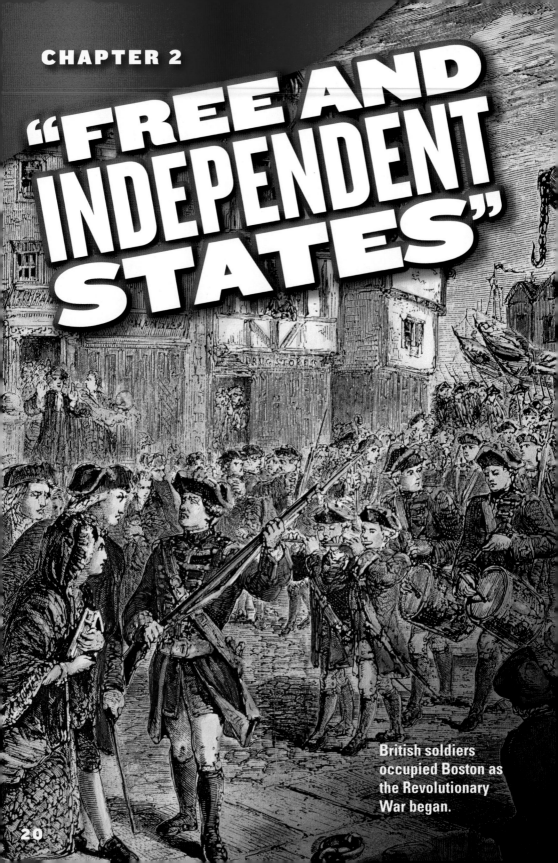

CHAPTER 2

"FREE AND INDEPENDENT STATES"

British soldiers occupied Boston as the Revolutionary War began.

ALTHOUGH THE FIRST SHOTS had been fired in the Revolutionary War, many colonists were not yet ready to separate from their home country. They considered themselves British. British trade had helped their businesses, and the British military had protected their homes. But a war had begun, and many Americans were inching toward the idea of independence.

In 1776, author Thomas Paine wrote a pamphlet called *Common Sense*, explaining why the American colonies should break away from Britain. The pamphlet quickly sold more than 150,000 copies. Paine's powerful arguments began a countrywide debate about the colonies' independence.

Breaking Ties

The Second Continental Congress began meeting in Philadelphia in May 1775. At a meeting of the Congress on June 7, 1776, Richard Henry Lee of Virginia offered this resolution: "That these United Colonies are, and of right ought to be, free and independent States, that they are absolved from all allegiance to the British Crown, and that all political connection between them and the State of Great Britain is, and ought to be, totally dissolved."

The delegates from seven colonies supported the resolution. The delegates from the other six colonies were not yet sure. Many wanted to write to officials back home to get instructions.

Richard Henry Lee was the first delegate to directly support a separation of the colonies from Great Britain.

(Left to right) Franklin, Jefferson, Livingston, Adams, and Sherman worked together to create the Declaration of Independence.

Meanwhile, the Continental Congress delegates decided that they should explain to the world why America was breaking its ties with Britain. They wanted to say more about why America was justified in declaring independence.

Congress appointed a committee of five men to write the Declaration of Independence. The five were John Adams of Massachusetts, Benjamin Franklin of Pennsylvania, Thomas Jefferson of Virginia, Robert Livingston of New York, and Roger Sherman of Connecticut.

The other members of the Declaration Committee had to convince Jefferson to write the first draft of the declaration.

Three Reasons

John Adams had no doubt about which member of the Declaration Committee should write the first draft: Thomas Jefferson. Jefferson, however, did not want the job. He thought Adams should write the declaration because Adams had been a main leader of the push for independence.

Adams refused, and he later recalled giving Jefferson three reasons why he should draft the declaration. "Reason, first, you are a Virginian, and a Virginian ought to appear at the head of this business." Virginia was the oldest, largest, and wealthiest of the 13 colonies.

Adams continued, "Reason second, I am obnoxious, suspected, and unpopular. You are very much otherwise." Adams did in fact have a reputation for being blunt and argumentative. Finally, Adams concluded, "Reason third, you can write ten times better than I."

The Author of the Declaration

Thomas Jefferson was 33 years old in the summer of 1776. He was one of the youngest members of the Continental Congress and one of the quietest. Jefferson seldom spoke in Congress. He could be painfully shy

Jefferson's draft became one of the foundations of the United States.

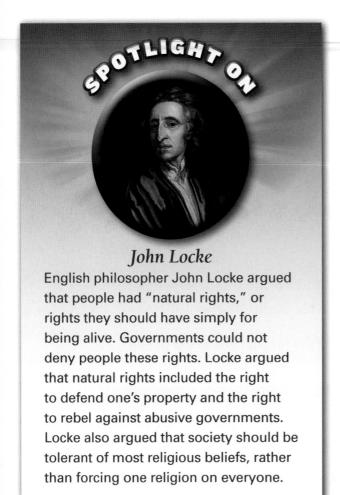

John Locke

English philosopher John Locke argued that people had "natural rights," or rights they should have simply for being alive. Governments could not deny people these rights. Locke argued that natural rights included the right to defend one's property and the right to rebel against abusive governments. Locke also argued that society should be tolerant of most religious beliefs, rather than forcing one religion on everyone.

and awkward. But everyone understood he was a remarkably skilled writer with a powerful mind.

Many members of the Continental Congress had read a paper Jefferson had written called "A Summary View of the Rights of British America." In it, he wrote that kings "are the servants" of people, not their owners. By this, he meant that the king's duty is to protect his subjects, not take advantage of them.

He also argued that people had the right to decide for themselves how they should be governed. "The God who gave us life," he wrote, "gave us liberty."

In the 1700s, many people were thinking about the nature of being human and the role of individuals in society and government. This period was known as the Enlightenment. Enlightenment thinkers celebrated reason, which human beings use to improve themselves and the world around them. In writing the declaration,

An original draft of the declaration shows how Jefferson wrote and revised his thoughts.

Jefferson was influenced by Enlightenment thought, particularly the works of philosopher John Locke.

Jefferson retreated to his rented rooms to write. Every morning, he sat down at his small desk. Slowly

A FIRSTHAND LOOK AT
AN EARLY DRAFT

Thomas Jefferson spent two weeks writing the Declaration of Independence. He wrote several drafts, polishing each one so that his words best expressed the colonists' desire for freedom. Some of Jefferson's early drafts still exist. Historians study the changes to see how Jefferson's thoughts evolved as he wrote the declaration. See page 60 for a link to view an early draft of the Declaration of Independence, with Jefferson's own handwritten changes, online.

The Continental Congress was impressed with the committee's work.

and painfully, the words came to him. He tore up some versions and changed many words.

At last, the declaration was ready to show to the other members of the Declaration Committee. Adams and Franklin made a few changes. Finally, the declaration was ready to present to the Continental Congress.

The Greatest Question

Before the Continental Congress considered the declaration, they first had to discuss Richard Henry

Lee's resolution about independence. On July 2, after much debate, 12 of the 13 colonies voted for independence. The delegates from New York had not yet been given instructions from the New York Assembly on how to vote, so they did not vote at all. Two weeks later, New York would add its vote in favor of the resolution.

The colonies had proclaimed that they were no longer part of Great Britain. "Yesterday, the greatest question was decided which ever was debated in America," John Adams wrote to his wife, Abigail. "A Resolution was passed without one **dissenting** Colony 'that these united Colonies are, and of right ought to be, free and independent States.'" Adams concluded, "It is the will of heaven that the two countries should be sundered [separated] forever."

SPOTLIGHT ON

Abigail Adams

Abigail Adams, wife of John Adams, was an active spokesperson in the cause of independence. While working with the Continental Congress in Philadelphia, John wrote many letters to Abigail in Massachusetts asking for her advice on political matters. She was strongly opposed to slavery and was an early supporter of women's rights, particularly regarding education and property rights. In a letter advising John as work on the declaration progressed, she urged him to "remember the ladies, and be more generous and favorable to them than your ancestors. Do not put such unlimited power into the hands of the Husbands."

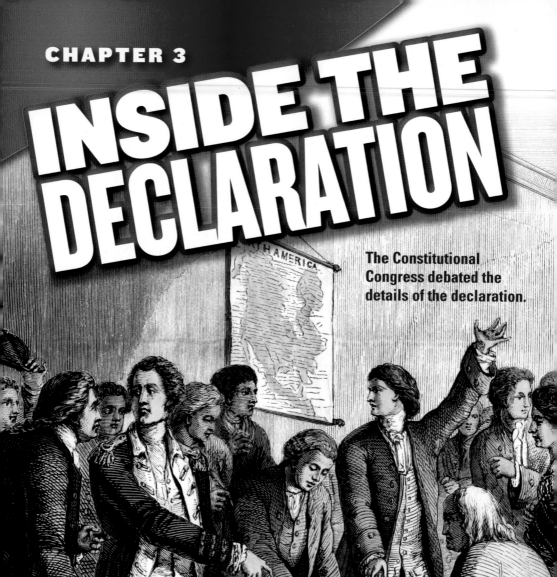

CHAPTER 3

INSIDE THE DECLARATION

The Constitutional Congress debated the details of the declaration.

THE COLONIES NOW HAD TO agree on the exact wording of the Declaration of Independence to properly explain to the world why they had announced their independence.

For three days, the delegates pored over Jefferson's draft of the declaration. Jefferson sat quietly while changes were suggested. He complained little, but he was miserable. The words that he had struggled over for two weeks were being altered. About 100 changes were made, and about one-quarter of Jefferson's words were eliminated.

Thomas Jefferson owned many slaves.

The Question of Slavery

The most hotly debated section of the document concerned slavery. In the draft of the declaration, Jefferson blamed the king for bringing slavery to America. "He has waged cruel war against human nature itself," Jefferson wrote, "violating its most sacred rights of life & liberty in the persons of a distant people who never offended him."

Some people found it strange that Jefferson had included this, because he owned slaves. More than 200 enslaved men, women, and children lived and worked at Monticello, Jefferson's home in Virginia. They tended his

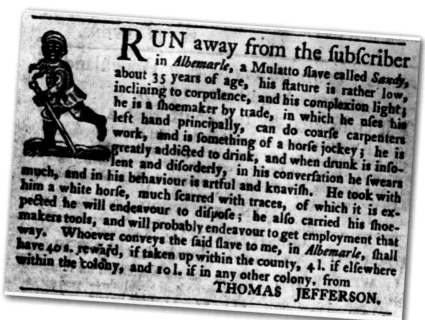

Jefferson's notice contained a description of his missing slave and an offer of a reward.

fields and cooked his meals. Though Jefferson relied on slavery to maintain his own way of life, he considered it an evil. "Nothing is more certainly written in the book of fate, than that these people are to be free," he wrote in 1821.

A FIRSTHAND LOOK AT
THOMAS JEFFERSON, SLAVE OWNER

Before the Revolutionary War, Jefferson proposed a plan in the Virginia Assembly to end slavery, but it did not get support. After the war, he tried to convince Congress to pass a law that would gradually end slavery, but it, too, failed. Despite this, Jefferson remained a slaveholder. In 1769, he put a notice in a Virginia newspaper, offering a reward for the return of one of his runaway slaves. See page 60 for a link to view the notice.

Slavery was central to the economy of the South. Delegates from southern states were not about to sign a document criticizing slavery. Some delegates from northern states also refused to denounce slavery. The slave trade had made them rich. The slave trade involved kidnapping people in Africa and shipping them to North America to be sold as slaves.

Many other delegates disapproved of slavery. Men such as Benjamin Franklin would have gladly kept the language criticizing the practice. But they thought it was more important to pass *some* version of the declaration, and do so quickly. They knew that the pro-slavery delegates would never agree to Jefferson's language. So they agreed to eliminate all mention of slavery from the document.

Slave labor was an important part of the southern agricultural economy.

Jefferson chose his words carefully as he wrote the declaration.

Rights and Charges

Despite the many changes that Congress had made to the document, the declaration remained Jefferson's words. Even the title was meaningful. At the top of the paper, Jefferson had written "The Unanimous Declaration of the Thirteen United States of America." The colonies had become "states."

Jefferson began the declaration by explaining why it had been written. "When in the Course of human events," he wrote, "it becomes necessary for one people to dissolve the political bands which have connected

The delegates wanted to make sure that the world knew exactly why they had chosen to break away from Great Britain.

them with another, . . . a decent respect to the opinions of mankind requires that they should declare the causes." Jefferson was saying that breaking away from Britain was such a large step that the world deserved to understand the reasons for it.

Next are the most quoted lines of the declaration: "We hold these truths to be self-evident, that all men are created equal, that they are endowed by their Creator with certain unalienable Rights, that among these are Life, Liberty and the pursuit of Happiness." In this section, Jefferson listed the most basic rights to which all people are entitled, just by being born.

When Jefferson talked about everyone being created equal, he did not mean that everyone is exactly the same. What he meant is that all people possess these most basic human rights and that everyone is equal in the eyes of the law. The government and the courts should treat a rich person and a poor person the same way.

Jefferson argued that no government can take away the rights to life, liberty, and the pursuit of happiness. In fact, Jefferson continued, the purpose of government is "to secure these rights." He explained that sometimes a government does not protect these rights. Sometimes a government treats people unfairly and limits liberty. When that happens, the people have the right to get rid of the government and start a new one. That, Jefferson explained, was the reason for the American Revolution.

Though the declaration stated that all men are created equal, enslaved people, women, and others were still not treated equally.

Unfair taxes such as the Stamp Act were one of the main reasons the declaration gave for the colonies separating from Great Britain.

Jefferson noted the ways in which the English king had trampled on the rights of Americans. He listed 27 charges against the king. They included that the king had "imposed taxes on us," "taken away our rights to a jury trial," and "waged war against us."

Jefferson concluded his document with a statement about American independence. The colonies, he said, are now "Free and Independent States" and "all political connection between them and the State of Great Britain, is and ought to be totally dissolved."

Hanging Together

On July 4, 1776, the Continental Congress held a vote on adopting the final version of the Declaration of Independence. It was approved by a **unanimous** vote.

Independence Hall

The delegates to the Continental Congress spent the hot summer of 1776 debating independence in a building now called Independence Hall. Prior to the American Revolution, the building served as the Pennsylvania State House. The members of the Continental Congress gathered in the building's small Assembly Room to pore over the declaration. Eleven years later, the U.S. Constitution was written in the same room.

The only delegate to sign the Declaration of Independence that day was John Hancock, the president of the Continental Congress. The other delegates did not sign until August 2. Hancock wrote his name in large, clear letters. According to one story, Hancock said he wrote his name extra large to make sure that King George could read it without his glasses. Hancock's signature is one of the most famous signatures in history.

John Hancock was the first delegate to sign the declaration.

It is so famous that a person's signature is sometimes called a John Hancock.

To the British, signing the declaration was an act of treason. Benjamin Franklin noted, "We must all hang together, or assuredly we will all hang separately." He was saying that if the Americans lost the war, the signers would be considered traitors. They would be put on trial and likely hanged for their crimes.

Hancock's signature stands out among those of the other delegates.

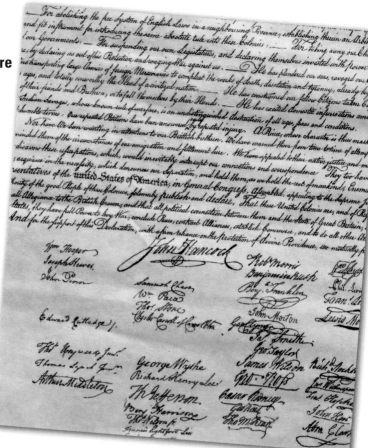

John Hancock attached a letter to the declaration and sent both documents to Governor Nicholas Cooke of Rhode Island. Hancock informed Cooke of the announcement of independence from Britain, writing, "The Congress have judged it necessary to dissolve all connection between Great Britain and the American Colonies, and to declare them free and independent States; as you will perceive by the enclosed Declaration, which I am directed to transmit to you." See page 60 for a link to view Hancock's original letter online.

CHAPTER 4

SPREADING THE NEWS

News of the declaration spread quickly throughout the colonies.

WHEN WORD WAS GIVEN THAT the declaration was approved, the bell in the steeple atop nearby Christ Church was rung, announcing to the city, and the world, that the United States had declared its independence.

The declaration was read aloud to large groups of colonists.

Independence

Copies of the declaration were printed immediately. Men on horseback galloped across the countryside, delivering one copy of the declaration to the assembly in each state. Riders raced from town to town with more copies. All across the land, the declaration was posted on walls and read in town squares. As the news spread, joyous shouts filled the air. Americans were free from British rule.

The news reached General George Washington, the commander of the American army, on July 9 in New York City. When the troops first heard the declaration, they threw their hats in the air. That night, proud Americans in New York City pulled down a lead statue of King George III on horseback. The statue was later melted down and turned into 42,000 bullets to be used during the Revolutionary War.

A VIEW FROM ABROAD

News of the Declaration of Independence enraged the British. Lord North, the prime minister of Great Britain, gave a man named John Lind the job of responding to the declaration. Lind's answer to the brief, one-page declaration was a 133-page pamphlet. Lind questioned how a slaveholder like Jefferson could write "all men are created equal" without freeing his own slaves.

English writer Jeremy Bentham said that if Americans' demands were based on any law, they would simply have to produce that law and there would be no argument. "Instead what do they produce?" Bentham scoffed. "What they call self-evident truths."

The War of Independence

The United States had declared its independence, but it still had to win it by defeating the well-trained, well-supplied British army. Thousands of British troops arrived on American shores. The Americans were short

The Marquis de Lafayette worked closely with George Washington during the Revolutionary War.

of food and supplies, and were not well trained in the early months of the war.

But slowly, the tide turned. Some people in Europe stepped forward to help the Americans. They believed in the cause of American freedom. Tadeusz Kościuszko of Poland and the Marquis de Lafayette of France provided military advice. France also provided money and troops.

In October 1781, after losing several key battles, the British surrendered and most of the fighting stopped. The official end of the war came with the signing of the Treaty of Paris in September 1783.

Echoes through the Years

The Declaration of Independence speaks to the highest hope of what the United States can and should be. Though the declaration says that all men are created equal, Americans have often not been treated equally.

At the time the declaration was written, women could not vote or hold political office. They were limited in what jobs they could hold. In 1848,

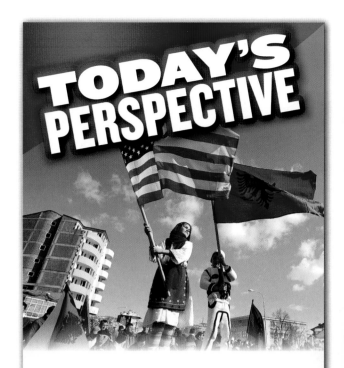

TODAY'S PERSPECTIVE

Many modern historians and writers believe that the Declaration of Independence was a **radical** statement regarding its view of government. Prior to the declaration, Europeans believed that governments existed to maintain order and protect society. The Declaration of Independence, however, claims that the main function of government is to protect the rights of the person. For the first time, it was the individual, and not society, that was considered the most important. Therefore, a government's success is not measured by how well society is protected, but by how free a person is.

The Seneca Falls Convention helped pave the way for women's rights.

women gathered in Seneca Falls, New York, for a women's rights convention. Elizabeth Cady Stanton, who had helped organize the convention, wrote a Declaration of Sentiments. In it, Stanton proclaimed, "We hold these truths to be self-evident, that all men and women are created equal." American women did not win the right to vote in all elections until 1920.

Nor had African Americans been treated as equals. Millions had been kept as slaves and treated as less than human. Even after slavery ended, black Americans were treated as if they were not as good as white Americans. In many parts of the country, black children were not allowed to go to the same schools as white children. In some parts of the country, white people kept black people from voting.

In university classrooms, black students often had to sit in separate rooms from white students.

In 1963, 250,000 people gathered in Washington, D.C., in support of protecting the civil rights of all Americans. On this day, civil rights leader Martin Luther King Jr. spoke about his vision of an America where people were not judged by the color of their skin. "I have a dream," he said, "that one day this nation will rise up and live out the true meaning of its creed—'we hold these truths to be self-evident, that *all* men are created equal.'"

Martin Luther King's speech in Washington, D.C., was one of the defining events of the civil rights movement.

The Declaration of Independence has been preserved over the years.

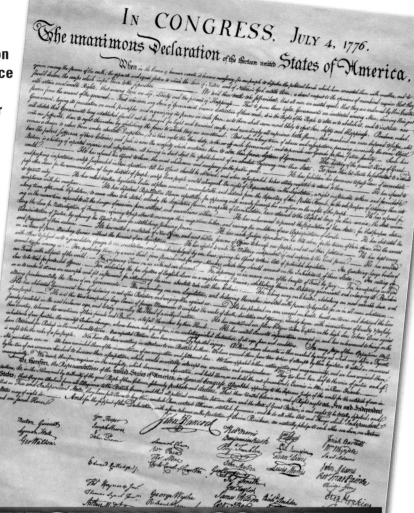

A FIRSTHAND LOOK AT
THE DECLARATION OF INDEPENDENCE

The copy of the Declaration of Independence signed by the delegates of the Continental Congress is on display at the National Archives in Washington, D.C. Each year, more than one million people visit the archives to see the document that gave birth to a nation. See page 60 for a link to view the original declaration and to read a transcript of its contents.

What Happened Where?

WI

...er the war, the declaration moved ...the capital of the young nation ...ved. First it was in New York ..., then Philadelphia, and finally ...shington, D.C.

IA

IL

IN

...ing the War of 1812, the British ...ned Washington, D.C., but ...ericans managed to quickly ...uggle the declaration out of town ...house in Leesburg, Virginia.

KS

MO

Fe...

K...

...ing World War II, people ...red that the Japanese military ...ht bomb Washington, D.C. The ...laration was carefully packed and ...ied to Fort Knox, Kentucky, the ...ce where the nation's supply of ...d is stored.

OK

AR

TN

TX

MS

AL

LA

Gulf of ...

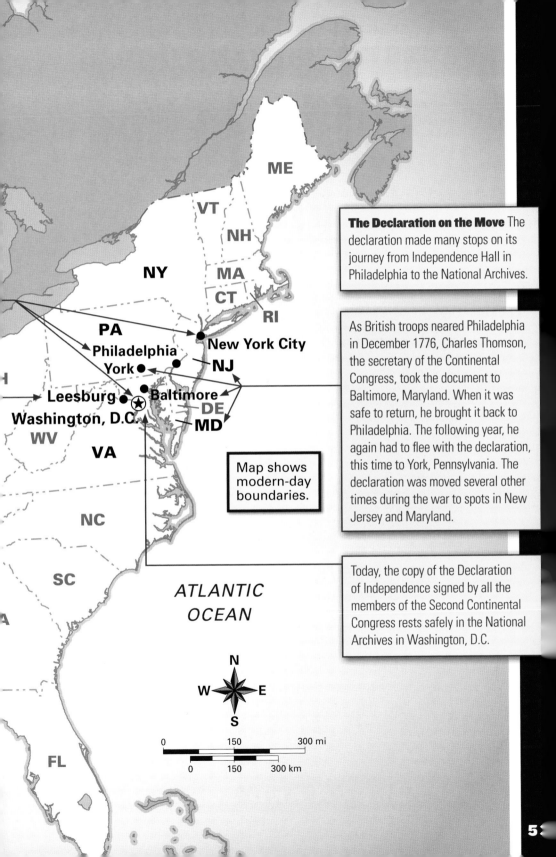

ME

VT

NH

NY

MA

CT

RI

PA

Philadelphia

York ●

New York City

NJ

Leesburg ● ●⊛

Baltimore

Washington, D.C.

DE

MD

WV

VA

NC

SC

FL

ATLANTIC
OCEAN

Map shows
modern-day
boundaries.

The Declaration on the Move The
declaration made many stops on its
journey from Independence Hall in
Philadelphia to the National Archives.

As British troops neared Philadelphia
in December 1776, Charles Thomson,
the secretary of the Continental
Congress, took the document to
Baltimore, Maryland. When it was
safe to return, he brought it back to
Philadelphia. The following year, he
again had to flee with the declaration,
this time to York, Pennsylvania. The
declaration was moved several other
times during the war to spots in New
Jersey and Maryland.

Today, the copy of the Declaration
of Independence signed by all the
members of the Second Continental
Congress rests safely in the National
Archives in Washington, D.C.

N
W   E
S

0   150   300 mi
0   150   300 km

A Gift to the Future

The Statue of Liberty is recognized worldwide as a symbol of American freedom.

Signing the Declaration of Independence did not instantly create a land where everyone was equal and free. Nearly two and a half centuries later, there is still work to do. The United States is a land of constant change. It is home to people of every race, religion, and nationality. Amid all this, thanks to the declaration, Americans have a clear goal for their country, something to work toward: liberty for all, equality for all.

More than 200 years after Thomas Jefferson wrote the declaration, his words retain their power to inspire. Each year, Americans pause to observe the anniversary of the day the United States declared its independence to the world. On the Fourth of July, Americans celebrate their good fortune to live in a land dedicated to the ideas that all people are created equal and are free to pursue whatever life they choose.

The founders of the United States risked their lives to create a nation committed to the ideal of liberty. Their Declaration of Independence was a gift to later generations. It remains alive and vital, and a true cause for celebration.

Americans celebrate Independence Day with fireworks displays.

BOTH DIED ON JULY 4, 1826.

INFLUENTIAL INDIVIDUALS

John Locke

Samuel Adams

John Locke (1632–1704) was an English philosopher and a leading figure in the Enlightenment. His writings influenced many of the leaders of the American Revolution.

Benjamin Franklin (1706–1790) was a scientist, statesman, printer, and inventor, and was one of the most influential founders of the United States. He represented Pennsylvania at the Second Continental Congress, but illness limited his participation in the Declaration Committee.

Samuel Adams (1722–1803) helped organize the Boston Tea Party and was a leader in the movement for independence.

John Adams (1735–1826) was a leading supporter of independence and a member of the Declaration Committee. He was elected second president of the United States.

Patrick Henry (1736–1799) was a politician who led the movement for independence in Virginia and fought with local colonists against the British and their Indian allies during the Revolutionary War.

John Hancock (1737–1793) was a merchant who served as president of the Second Continental Congress.

Thomas Paine (1737–1809) was the author of *Common Sense*, a pamphlet that helped convince many Americans that independence from Britain was a good idea.

King George III (1738–1820) was the king of Great Britain in the years leading to and during the Revolutionary War.

Thomas Jefferson (1743–1826) was the primary author of the Declaration of Independence. He was elected the third president of the United States.

Abigail Adams (1744–1818) was the wife of John Adams who offered political advice to her husband in a series of letters they exchanged while he worked on the declaration. She was a strong supporter of women's rights and an opponent of slavery.

Abigail Adams

Elizabeth Cady Stanton (1815–1902) was a leader of the early women's rights movement. She worked to gain voting rights for women. She was also concerned with women's property rights and employment rights, and with family law.

Martin Luther King Jr. (1929–1968) was a minister and a leading figure of the civil rights movement of the 1950s and 1960s. In 1963, he delivered his "I Have a Dream" speech in Washington, D.C.

TIMELINE

1607

English colonists begin setting up permanent colonies in North America.

1763

The French and Indian War ends, leaving Great Britain in debt.

1765

The British Parliament passes the Stamp Act, putting a tax on printed materials.

1773

Americans dump 342 chests of tea into Boston Harbor to protest the tax on tea.

1774

Parliament passes the Intolerable Acts, placing Massachusetts under military rule and closing Boston Harbor.

1775

The first battles of the American Revolutionary War are fought at Lexington and Concord in Massachusetts.

1766

Parliament repeals the Stamp Act.

1767

Parliament passes a tax on tea, glass, paper, and other goods.

1770

British soldiers kill five Americans in the Boston Massacre.

1776

The Second Continental Congress approves the Declaration of Independence.

1783

The Revolutionary War ends.

LIVING HISTORY

Primary sources provide firsthand evidence about a topic. Witnesses to a historical event create primary sources. They include autobiographies, newspaper reports of the time, oral histories, photographs, and memoirs. A secondary source analyzes primary sources, and is one step or more removed from the event. Secondary sources include textbooks, encyclopedias, and commentaries.

Boston Tea Party Engraving To see W. D. Cooper's well-known print, *Boston Tea Party*, published in 1789, go to *www.loc.gov /exhibits/british/images/vc40.jpg*

The Declaration of Independence To view the original Declaration of Independence signed by the delegates of the Second Continental Congress, go to *www.archives.gov/exhibits/charters /declaration_zoom_1.html*

An Early Draft of the Declaration of Independence Several of Thomas Jefferson's original drafts of the declaration still exist. To view one of his drafts and see the changes he made to his work, go to *www.ushistory.org/declaration/document/rough.htm*

A John Hancock Letter To read John Hancock's letter to Rhode Island governor Nicholas Cooke announcing the signing of the declaration and requesting him to build ships to defend the new nation, go to *www.indiana.edu/~liblilly/history/history4.html*

Thomas Jefferson, Slave Owner To view an advertisement that Jefferson ran in a Virginia newspaper seeking the return of one of his slaves, go to *www.loc.gov/exhibits/jefferson/images/vc37.jpg*

Books

Aronson, Marc. *The Real Revolution: The Global Story of American Independence*. New York: Clarion Books, 2005.

Ching, Jacqueline. *Thomas Jefferson*. New York: DK Publishing, 2009.

Freedman, Russell. *Give Me Liberty! The Story of the Declaration of Independence*. New York: Holiday House, 2000.

Kimmel, Heidi. *The Battles of Lexington and Concord*. New York: Children's Press, 2007.

Mullin, Rita T. *Thomas Jefferson: Architect of Freedom*. New York: Sterling, 2007.

Yero, Judith Lloyd. *The Declaration of Independence*. Washington, D.C.: National Geographic, 2006.

Web Sites

Independence National Historical Park
www.nps.gov/inde/index.htm
Visitors can see Independence Hall, where the Continental Congress debated the Declaration of Independence.

Library of Congress—Creating the Declaration of Independence
http://myloc.gov/Exhibitions/creatingtheus/DeclarationofIndependence/Pages/default.aspx
Check out one of the Internet's best sites on U.S. history and the Declaration of Independence.

National Archives—Charters of Freedom: Declaration of Independence
www.archives.gov/exhibits/charters/declaration.html
View prints of the Declaration of Independence and the original document. Learn how it was written and is being preserved.

GLOSSARY

assembly (uh-SEM-blee) a lawmaking body

boycott (BOI-kaht) refusing to buy goods from a person, group, or country

broadsides (BRAWD-sides) posters; large sheets of paper printed on one side

colonists (KAH-luh-nists) people who settle in a new land but continue to be ruled by the government from their old country

debt (DET) money or something else that someone owes

delegates (DEL-i-gitz) representatives to a convention or congress

dissenting (di-SENT-ing) disagreeing with or opposing an idea or opinion

intolerable (in-TOL-ur-uh-buhl) unbearable

Parliament (PAR-luh-muhnt) the part of the British government that makes laws

radical (RAD-i-kuhl) thorough and with a wide range of important effects

Redcoats (RED-kotes) British soldiers during the time of the American Revolutionary War

repeal (ri-PEEL) the act of officially doing away with something

resolution (rez-uh-LOO-shuhn) a declaration adopted by a legislative body

treason (TREE-zuhn) the crime of betraying one's own country

unanimous (yoo-NAN-uh-muhss) with everyone in agreement

veto (VEE-toh) to stop a bill from becoming a law

INDEX

Page numbers in *italics* indicate illustrations.

Adams, Abigail, 29, *29*, 57, *57*
Adams, John, 17, 23, *23*, 24–25, 28, 29, 56
Adams, Samuel, 17, 18, *18*, 56, *56*
African Americans, 49–50, *49*, *50*
assemblies, 6–7, 9, 29, 33, 39, 44
Attucks, Crispus, 14

Bentham, Jeremy, 45
Boston Harbor, 16, 17
Boston, Massachusetts, 13–14, 17, *20*
Boston Massacre, 13–14, *14*, 15, *15*
Boston Tea Party, 16–17, *16*, 18
Boston Tea Party (W. D. Cooper), 17
British military, 13–14, *14*, 15, 17, 18, 19, *19*, *20*, 21, 45, 47, 52, 53
broadsides, 15, *15*

Christ Church, *42*, 43
civil rights movement, 49–50, *49*, *50*, 57
colonies, 7, *8*, 9, 10, 13, 14, *14*, 18, 21, 24, 29, 31, 35, 39, 41, *42*
colonists, 7, 9, 10, 11, *11*, 12, 13–14, *14*, 16, *16*, 17, 18, 21, 27, 44–45, *44*, 56
Common Sense (Thomas Paine), 21, 57
Concord, Massachusetts, 18, 19
Continental army, *19*, 45–46, 56
Continental Congress, 18, 22, 23, 25, 26, 28–29, *28*, *30*, 33, 35, 39, 41, 51, 52, 56
Cooke, Nicholas, 41
Cooper, W. D., 17
copies, 44, *44*, 51, *51*, 53

Declaration Committee, 23, *23*, 24, *24*, 28, *28*, 56
Declaration of Sentiments, 48
delegates, 18, 22, *22*, 23, 25, 31, 34, *36*, 39–41, *40*, 51
drafts, 18, 24, *24*, *25*, 27–28, *27*, 31, 32, 57

economy, 34, *34*
Enlightenment period, 26–27, 56
equality, 36, 37–38, *37*, 45, 47, 48, 49, 50, 54, *54*, 55

Fort Knox, 52
France, 10, *10*, 46–47, *46*
Franklin, Benjamin, 23, *23*, 28, 34, 40–41, 56

French and Indian War, 10–11, *10*

George III, king of England, 7, 11, 17, 18, 26, 32, 38, 39, 40, 45, 57
governors, 9, 16, 41
Great Britain, 6–7, 9, 10–11, *10*, 12–13, *13*, 13–14, *14*, 15, 16, 17, 18, 19, *19*, *20*, 21, 22, 23, 26, 29, 36, 39, 40, 41, 45, 47, 52, 53, 56, 57

Hancock, John, 39–40, *40*, 41, *41*, 56
Henry, Patrick, 6, *6*, 7, 56
human rights. *See* equality.

"I Have a Dream" speech, 50, *50*, 57
Independence Day, 55, *55*
Independence Hall, 39, *39*, 53
Intolerable Acts, 17, 18

Jefferson, Thomas, 18, 23, *23*, 24–25, *24*, 25–26, *25*, 27–28, *27*, 31, 32, *32*, 33, *33*, 34, 35, *35*, 36, 37–38, 39, 45, 54–55, 57

King, Martin Luther, Jr., 50, *50*, 57
Kościuszko, Tadeusz, 46

Lafayette, Marquis de, 46, *46*
laws, 7, 9, 17, 33, 37, 45
Lee, Richard Henry, 22, *22*, 28–29
Lexington, Massachusetts, 19, *19*
Lind, John, 45
Livingston, Robert, 23, *23*
Locke, John, 26, *26*, 27, 56, *56*

map, *52–53*

National Archives, 51, 53
news, 7, 14, *42*, 44–45
newspapers, 11, 15, 33, *33*
North, Lord, 45

Paine, Thomas, 21, 57
Parker, John, 19
Parliament, 6–7, 11, 12, 17, 18
Pennsylvania State House. *See* Independence Hall.
Philadelphia, Pennsylvania, 18, 22, 29, 52, 53
Pitt, William, 13, *13*

presidents, 17, 39, 56, 57
protests, *11*, 12, *12*, 13, *16*, 17, 18, *38*

Revolutionary War, 7, 19, *19*, *20*, 21, 37,
    38, 39, 45, *46*, 56, 57
Richardson, Ebenezer, 15

Seneca Falls Convention, 48, *48*
Sherman, Roger, 23, *23*
signatures, 39–41, *40*, 41, *41*, 51, *51*, 53
slavery, 9, 29, 32–34, *32*, *33*, *34*, *37*, 45,
    49, 57
Stamp Act (1765), 6–7, 11–12, *11*, *12*, *38*
Stanton, Elizabeth Cady, 48, 57
"A Summary View of the Rights of British
    America" (Thomas Jefferson), 26

surrender, 47

taxes, 6–7, 11–12, *11*, *12*, 13, 16, 18, 38,
    38
tea, 13, 16, *16*, 17
Thomson, Charles, 53
Treaty of Paris, 47

voting rights, 47, 48, *48*, 49, 57

War of 1812, 52
Washington, D.C., 50, *50*, 51, 52, 53, 57
Washington, George, 45, *46*
women's rights, 29, 47–48, *48*, 57
World War II, 52

ABOUT THE AUTHOR

Melissa McDaniel is a writer and editor who grew up in Portland, Oregon. She graduated from Portland State University with a degree in history, specializing in the American colonial era. She also has a master's degree in library science from the University of Washington. McDaniel has written books for young people on subjects ranging from Ellis Island to the Powhatan Indians to life on the deep-sea floor. She lives in New York City with her husband, daughter, dog, and frog.

BRINGING HISTORY to LIFE

The Declaration of Independence marked the official separation of the American colonies from Great Britain.

Read about the events surrounding the creation of the Declaration of Independence and find out how the results of this historic document have shaped our nation today. Inside you will find out:

★ Why the American colonists wanted independence from Great Britain;

★ Why Thomas Jefferson was chosen to write the Declaration;

★ And how Great Britain responded when the colonies declared independence.

Cornerstones of Freedom™ brings history to life by capturing the dramatic and defining moments in American history with engaging text, primary source materials, historical photographs, maps, and timelines.

ISBN-13: 978-0-531-26555-0
ISBN-10: 0-531-26555-2
90000

Children's Press®
an imprint of

■SCHOLASTIC

www.scholastic.com/librarypublishing

U.S. $8.95

9 780531 265550